Secure the Shadow

SOUTHERN MESSENGER POETS

Dave Smith, Series Editor

Secure the Shadow

POEMS

CLAUDIA EMERSON

LOUISIANA STATE UNIVERSITY PRESS

BATON ROUGE

Published by Louisiana State University Press
Copyright © 2012 by Claudia Emerson
All rights reserved
Manufactured in the United States of America

DESIGNER: Barbara Neely Bourgoyne
TYPEFACE: Whitman

LIBRARY OF CONGRESS CATALOGING-IN-PUBLICATION DATA

Emerson, Claudia, 1957–
    Secure the shadow : poems / Claudia Emerson.
        p. cm. — (Southern messenger poets)
    ISBN 978-0-8071-4303-2 (pbk. : alk. paper) — ISBN 978-0-8071-4302-5 (cloth : alk. paper) — ISBN
978-0-8071-4304-9 (pdf) — ISBN 978-0-8071-4305-6 (epub) — ISBN 978-0-8071-4306-3 (mobi)
    I. Title.
    PS3551.N4155S43 2012
    811'.54—dc22

                                                                                2011023197

Many thanks to the editors of the following magazines, in which these poems first appeared:
Birmingham Poetry Review: "First Death," "*I*," "The Porch," and "The Present Tense"; *Blackbird:*
"Secure the Shadow"; *Boulevard:* "Half-Life: Pittsylvania County, Virginia" and "Dial Variations";
Connotation Press, an Online Artifact: "Variations from the Porch"; *Dead Mule School of Southern
Literature:* "Documentary" (published as "Collective: A Drift of Hogs"); *Elder Mountain:* "Arterial"
and "For Once"; *Hopkins Review:* "Jubilation," "The Hearing," and "After Hours: A Glimpse of the
Radiologist"; *The New Yorker:* "Catfish"; *New York Times:* "Elegy in July for the Motel Astra"; *Poetry
East:* "Then" (published as "Night Shift"), "Cold Room," "Refusal" (published as "The Spoon"), and
"Zenith"; *Prairie Schooner:* "Student Conference," "Lifeguard," "Late April House Fire along Interstate
81," and "Namesake"; *Southern Spaces:* "Old Elementary"; *Tar River Poetry:* "Animal Funerals, 1964";
Valparaiso Poetry Review: "Ground Truth" and "Vacancy."

    For unwavering support while writing this book, the author gives lasting thanks to her family
and her husband, Kent Ippolito; friends and colleagues Betty Adcock, Judith Harris, Carole Garmon,
Andrew Hudgins, Catherine MacDonald, Danny and Linda Marion, Mara Scanlon, Rod Smith, and
David Wojahn; and the Virginia Center for the Creative Arts for two residencies.

For my brother and my father in memory

Memory believes before knowing remembers.

—WILLIAM FAULKNER

Contents

I

Late April House Fire along Interstate 81

I had wondered for some time about its source,
       the smoke a fixed-roiling column visible

for miles, unchanged by the wind
       that had all day blown across the road

with pollen and bees a fine spring snow
       salting fields newly greening, the redbuds

livid beneath it. By the time I came upon it,
       fire was indivisible part of the two-story,

woodframe farm house—still itself, completely
       whole, composed: white clapboard, porch and roof,

front door, window frames—glass panes intact—
       the chimneys that would survive, calm inside

the flames' straight rush—contained, bright-rising
       enravishment. I knew this was nothing

like the worse resolve of another hour
       when the backward gravity of fire

would have relented to the old habit
       of collapse, the sift of slow ash down

on all that does not burn—hinges, latches,
       doorknobs, keys still sunk in the locks, the wind

passing through windowless air. But this was
       anguish not yet grief. And so I slowed

but did not stop to watch someone else's
       tragedy burn past this brief, nearly

beautiful suspension that changes nothing.

Half-Life: Pittsylvania County, Virginia

CHATHAM, VA., JANUARY 2, 2008—Underneath a plot of farmland used
to raise cattle, hay, and timber in south-central Virginia lies what is thought
to be the largest deposit of uranium in the United States.

Uranium was discovered by eighteenth-century chemist Martin Heinrich
Klaproth, who called it "a strange kind of half-metal" and named it in part
for the recently discovered seventh planet, Uranus, one of the so-called
"ice giants."

That some slow, cold distant planet formed
        with a core of ice and stone and named
for the embodiment of sky and heaven
        should have anything to do with it seemed wrong—
given its rumored rise from pitchblende to the surface
        of fields and pastures, its dissolve into the wells
dug and the ponds made for the animals,
        or its decay into the brief, more deadly

daughters—an old explosion's persistent, widening
        wake—and now even more wrong given its ungodly
worth to the men who had already sold
        the rights to it, ignorant of the worse cost
of confusing what chooses us with what we choose,
        the near-infinite half-life of remains.

        •

And the worry that cancer simply ran
        in families had been replaced by suspicion
of a greater cause: the massive vein
        of uranium found just a few miles
outside of town on farms where in the 1950s
        scientists had come to look because
of a known fault, restless in the rock.
        The percussive, intermittent *tick*

of their Geiger counters had escalated
        to something measureless—the place itself
a worse genetic element, the very land
        guilty. In the small sanctuary
of the Presbyterian church where I was raised—
        the women's whispering soft and steady
as the beat of moths' wings—their purses
        still closed around tissues, lozenges, the same

thin tithes and offerings. Among them, I could recount
        losses so common it was no wonder
they had come after time to believe
        predestined sacrifice: of the easily
stricken elderly, or a son in middle age,
        an infant or toddler daughter.

The cancers: both common and rare—
        of the lung, stomach, brain, pancreas, liver,
breast, of the ovary, the blood itself,
        the houses on the street where I grew up
marked with its slow plague—patient,
        insatiable—not one passed over.

                    ◆

My father recalled a story about a family
        who lived in the oldest house on some of that land,
the structure built of brick, slave-made on the place,
        he said, of the place itself—and about one
of the women stricken with a tumor of the brain
        before there was an instrument to see it,
long before anyone knew what uranium was.
        The story misremembered, half-lie

or whole, I imagined again that house,
        her body-driven madness appearing
first as headache—the one pupil eclipsing

its iris before auras around the windows,
around the children's heads, the chimney ciphering
        like the church organ pipe, one long note

unplayed, the sound unaccounted for. She would have been
        bound inside herself to a stake—burning at it,
the rope around her wrists giving way a little
        every day to the stronger bonds of invisible fire;
what if it were in the walls, the brick laced with it,
        the water, the melons and eggs, the milk; what if

she sifted it with the salt into the flour and fried it
        in the pan, telling her daughter to run away
from her, to go, *you go, every day,*
        as far as you can. But what if it were
in her apron with her little knife;
        she could see clearly herself in its blade.

                    ◆

We had already memorized the three-bladed
        black fan, symbol for the fallout shelter
the men had built under the post office,
        beneath its thick-combed walls of letter boxes—
small-windowed, gilt-numbered doors with bronze
        combinations we would inherit,
thresholds opening to promise and debt.
        It was somewhere beneath the cases

where the rural carriers sorted their routes,
        long days of gravel back roads, orbits
relentless, the sinuous dust of retraces.
        I never saw that shelter, never met
anyone who had, but believed in deep shelves
        of syrupy pears and peaches as I had been taught
to believe in heaven, safe, dreaded
        place I was told I would go, not meaning

for my soul to be taken in my sleep,
        not meaning to drift past the moon, past
the farthest planets, the slow, dim one ringed
        with dust and ice. It glowed the palest green
of opaque glass, a globe at the end
        of an empty street, so far from the source
it appeared bioluminescent origin,
        half cause, half sanctuary of last light.

Student Conference

At first, I mistook the small, black tattoo
    for a phone number or a date jotted

in haste on her wrist's paler underside—
    then suspected stitches when it didn't fade.

I was not far wrong. (Her poems: careful,
    deliberate, thin as she was, haunted by a mother

years dead—not a word about the brief grief
    of the father who saw in her a worsening

resemblance.) I imagined what it took
    for her to enter the parlor, where nothing—

garish bird, snake, broken heart—could tempt her,
    turn her from the small, determined letters:

think. The word she had purchased moved faintly
    in what she must have thought would be

permanence above her pulse, her body's argument
    to think what she wished she could still feel,

arm bared for another coming
    into being, the needle's indelible sting.

Elegy in July for the Motel Astra

The desolation without season, summer
        somehow heightens it, Route 1's course from Maine
to Florida interstate-strangled, this narrow
        stretch in Virginia wasted as a riverbed
drought-hushed. Remains of gas stations, diners,
        and motels litter it, and here, July, long
month that had meant their greatest thriving,
        offers itself again to the decades' abandonment.

The motel signs, once neon sculptures
        of lyric light and promise, still advertise
darkly what was: *Corona, Radiant,*
        Starlight, Aurora, places named for skybound
destinations someone dreamed up to lure those
        on their way to or from the ocean,
to or from the mundane everyday,
        the heat, at least for a time—a night—escapable.

A place or two are still rented by the season
        to migrant workers following a harvest,
tobacco, peanuts, soybeans—or the paving
        of other roads. But most have fallen beyond use,
windows paneless, still-numbered doors ajar,
        anything worth salvage hauled out piecemeal,
the only inhabitants small birds, black snakes,
        wasps, and vines, cavity-seekers, their shadows.

From here, when the interstate stalls, the horizon glows
        past sunset—the convergence of brakelights and lowbeams
rising with the smell of sour crude oil and tar: jaundiced-rose
        fuming exhaust cast off as though from slow-
certain rage. And when the interstate is in motion, the sound
        of shifting gears and engine braking becomes
that of a storm, never quite formed,
        its forming ceaseless, thunder dry, impotent.

The Astra lingers on as a flea market
     and fruit stand, as though in a demented dream
of itself, some rooms filled with the detritus
     of what didn't sell at auction, some with fresher
produce: watermelons, tomatoes,
     cantaloupes, peaches warm to the touch.

The sign at the open gate of the swimming pool
     warns *no lifeguard*; the risk is yours. The owner
might have drained it, or let it drain itself,
     evaporate from precious clarity
to airless pond before this measured void,
     the diving board a dull, more deadly blade.

On the concrete floor of the pool, the years' collection
     of leaf rot, dust, rainfall and frost, the crickets
and toads that fell into and then could not
     escape it—have recomposed to form
the barest layer of soil. Strict plot, unruly,
     vagrant narrative. The poorest, most ordinary
plants volunteer, take shallow root, and fireflies
     seed the sunken air. The road took with it

the unreachable looming, the mirage's
     vivid shimmering above fresh blacktop
a shining unattainable refraction,
     a vision disappearing quick as the light
sweet crude we used to chase it—irresistible,
     that fleet mirror of what was sky.

It

My cousin liked to dangle me upside down
       by the ankles, my aunt's crossed in thick disapproval

at eye level, the world gone wrong, blood fallen
       in a dizzy rush to my ears until, almost

made afraid, I heard his familiar laughter
       as though from some sealed depth beneath me.

Until he is called up,
       Vietnam is sound

broadcast: the voice of evening
       news a televised census

of the dead, the rising number
       bodiless, somehow, nameless

narcosis of fact. Or it
       is still, in black and white:

water buffalo, the sullen
       work of drowned fields;

a monk sitting cross-legged
       in placid meditation

of the self as fire, eyes
       and mouth closed-calm part of it.

The doll arrived at Christmastime, halfway
       through my cousin's first tour of duty,

addressed to me, the narrow cardboard box
       decorated with delicate chrysanthemums,

her face visible beneath a pale caul
        of tissue paper. I lifted her out,

delighted with her strangeness, her red dress
        of real silk slit at the sides to the hip,

her conical grass hat. But I could imagine
        no part for her in the plots of my other dolls,

no dream house or car, no man. She was sewn
        tight into her only dress, her form,

a full grown woman's, rigid inside it, posture
        strict, unbending, her gaze untranslatable.

She had traveled across the ocean in the belly
        of a plane, in dark storage with letters, packages,

those flagged caskets. She was not dead, I decided,
        but made blind, and with no way to tell it,

no tongue in her mouth, her body hollow, soundless.

And then it is children
        running toward me, the faint,

rain-shimmering shadows before them
        stunted, those of early

afternoon, and a girl, naked,
        the scorched disfigurement

of her back unseen, inescapable
        as what had been the road

behind her, its vanishing point
        consumed inside an earthbound

cloud, her scream—seared
       aperture to something

the image cannot document.

The small box of ashes neatly buried,
       my cousin would drive me home

from my father's funeral, that mile
       the only conversation I would be able

to recall between the two of us alone,
       his summer visits for years brief and shallow—

the distance easy to blame. He would be
       matter of fact, telling me about

the Agent Orange he'd breathed, believed revenant
       in a tumor, the cancer in his throat—

its remission. Not a day had passed
       when he hadn't smelled it, tasted it—

the *it* slender and exact as a compass needle—
       he would say as though to the road ahead,

or suddenly blind to it, his eyes, tongue, throat,
       his voice I would hear burning with

a knowing beyond memory—wordless,
       imageless—the body's own account.

Secure the Shadow

Secure the shadow 'ere the substance fade

> —a popular daguerreotypist's advertising slogan for the
> making of postmortem images of loved ones

1.

It appears at first glance to be an infant
      asleep before the fact of death is clear:
a boy who still looks like a girl—the mother
      loath to cut his light fine hair—laid out
on a couch, its back of ornate, dark-carved wood
      all there is of the room, which very well
could have been the photographer's studio
      she had traveled to—how far?—with the body.

The photograph contains the whole of it:
      he wears a white gown that might have been
for the christening, no shoes, his plump hands
      posed, folded, dimpled, the hands
of a healthy child, the face still round with baby fat.
      Whatever took him, then, took him quickly—

whooping cough, pneumonia, a fever,
      something common that left no mark, and while
the posture is of sleep, the heavy-lidded
      inward gaze of the eyes, not quite closed,
makes no pretense of it. The mother might have lived
      to be one of the women expressionless
in other photographs. She might have borne

other children who lived and in surviving her
      let go this image they must have feared. And so
with some reluctance, I purchase its further
      removal from them, from her—making mine
this orphaned but still secure correspondence
      with all that is about to disappear.

2.

The caption's rough cursive records that the girl
        in the photograph has been dead nine days,
the mother refusing to part with her only daughter—
        the rigor having come and gone, the body
posed seated, posture flawless—head turned
        so that she gazes away slightly to her left,
at something just beyond the gold-embossed
        frame in thoughtful enthrallment. Nine days

since the first night of this, the bathing, viewing,
        and then the desperate bed of ice, until
the mother at last succumbed to insist on this
        familiar: a book in her daughter's right hand,
her left thumb holding down the page, place marked
        as though in a passage to which she will return.

3.

The photographer may not enter this house,
        the boy dead from scarlet fever, so the closed
window also frames the body, shutters
        open wide as though for light. He lies
on top of the made bed, wearing his winter
        jacket and a scarf, hair neatly combed, face toward
the lens, even as his gaze disobeys, as though intent on
        the stubborn sky instead, refusing this.

4.

This one a stereocard, the girl
        appears to the naked eye doubled, lying
on her side in a bed all white, beneath
        a dark-filled window curtained with delicate lace.
In her arms a cat, quite alive and nervous—
        mouth open—blurs its face in the turning,
about to escape this embrace made strange.
        Around its neck—the bell she had fastened,

to keep safe the birds she might have loved
in equal measure, perhaps, or merely
decorative, the small cheerful sounding
of return, the smaller sound of vanishing.

5.

Some of the youngest children have wasted
into the appearance of the very old,
the simple failure to thrive common
as it is irreversible, and so there was time
for a photograph before as well, taken
with toys, a rocking horse or doll, a wicker
carriage or favorite pair of shoes—one child
posed in a high chair with a bowl and spoon.

And some have their hands tied as though in bondage;
this is, the photographer's notes instruct,
to prevent displacement, the body's slow-
certain restlessness that does not die.

6.

Infant twins in a shared casket, the mother
and child, the living brother made to pose
touching the shoulder of the other. Too many,
then, for such close study: like the alive,
they become alike, or of a type.
There are, after all, only so many frames—
rooms and windows, cradles and caskets
encased within these smaller chambers crafted

of gold, silver, of skeletal leaves, only
so many ways to look until the light
changes, fades, is lost, the pane—the lens—
darkening from glass to mirror, until
the substance of the eye sees itself
outside the self, and then can look no further.

After Hours: A Glimpse of the Radiologist

Behind the seamless window that is
    the café's outer wall, he faces

his wife over a small, candlelit table,
    a white-aproned waiter moving—intent,

unnoticed—around them. The sidewalk
    and streetlights frame their late supper, begun

for him with a squat glass of merlot,
    I'd guess by the stouter stem, the dark

wine thick. The flute slender and tall, hers
    is more certainly champagne—the bead

I can see streaming clearly from here,
    despite the light fall of mist forming

on the glass between us. All day, he has been reading
    films and ultrasounds, x-rays, scans—looking

inside our bodies—gray-marbled breasts
    sequenced by shadowy lungs and hearts,

the rarer brain, a hand's delicate bones
    rendered into translucence. In this moment,

though, he pauses to offer a toast—to her,
    I imagine, and to the most ordinary survival

of a long week, or, perhaps, to the routine *nothing*
    here of any interest he has had the unusual

pleasure to say all day, becoming beautiful
    and absolute, the *nothing here at all.*

II

Animal Funerals, 1964

That summer, we did not simply walk through
    the valley of the shadow of death;

we set up camp there, orchestrating funerals
    for the anonymous, found dead: a drowned mole—

its small, naked palms still pink—a crushed
    box turtle, black snake, even a lowly toad.

The last and most elaborate of the burials—
    a common jay, identifiable

but light, dry, its eyes vacant orbits.
    We built a delicate lychgate of willow fronds,

supple and green, laced through with chains of clover.
    Roles were cast: preacher, undertaker—

the rest of us a straggling congregation
    reciting what we could of the psalm

about green pastures as we lowered the shoebox
    and its wilted pall of dandelions

into the shallow grave one of us had dug
    with a serving spoon. That afternoon,

just before September and school, when we would
    again become children, and blind to all

but the blackboard's chalky lessons, the back
    of someone's head, and what was, for a while

longer, the rarer, human death—there, in the heat-shimmered
    trees, in the matted grasses where we stood,

even in the slant of humid shade, we heard wingbeat,
    slither, buzz, and birdsong, a green racket rising

to fall as though in a sublime dirge that was real,
    and not part of our many necessary rehearsals.

First Death

Now, the first of my father's maiden aunts
      was dying, the frail kindest of the three,

her bed set up downstairs in the formal parlor
      where the coffin soon would follow, the room

darkened, curtains drawn against the day
      for no good reason I could see, an afternoon's

wasting outside equally terrible,
      all inside now defined by the other

aunts' hushed fussing, the smell of her breathing,
      of cloves, pain, of something unidentifiable

just beneath her nightgown, the soft veneer
      of talcum's dissolve. My mother asked me

to crush ice, something useful, she said,
      but I saw in it a way out as I wrestled cubes

from aluminum trays, wrapped them in a dishcloth
      to crush on the concrete stoop out back.

Alone then with the fattening shadows of sheets
      on the line, the sickbed filled with wind, I fell

to my task, sudden unfamiliar delight
      in the heft of the hammer, in a sound

as of bones breaking, the sense perhaps of some part
      giving way, a finger, maybe, a tooth,

fragile hand, delicate foot. I opened
      the cloth to dainty slivers I swaddled again

for her forehead, saving some, as I had been
           instructed, in a china cup, for her to hold

in her mouth. My mother took it from me,
           and from the threshold, I could see

my great-aunt's face abstracted in half-light,
           her mouth a deeper shadow closing—

what she might have understood
           of my labor already vanished on her tongue.

Zenith

Younger sister he suffers, I have just turned three,
        eating supper with my brother: in the photograph

he wears cowboy boots, dungarees, pajama top—
        his head shaved close to bald, six-shooter holstered

at the small table we share every night.
        I am also in boots, hand-me-down rifle

at the ready by my plate. My helmet
        from another war, its netting I'll weave

with leaves, broomsedge, pine fronds, anything
        to camouflage me, confuse the enemy

the way he has taught me, whispering *listen,*
        there, listen—Japanese, Germans, Apaches,

Yankees unseen, everywhere. We don't know
        how little we have to fear in our small

country town, for years its one traffic light
        a mere yellow pulse benign as a firefly's.

The enemies of this place—drought, hail, an early
        or late frost—refuse our aim, the smallest

human industry defined by the health
        of tobacco fluming in the fields that surround us.

I can't tell what's on our plates, but if it's Monday,
        meatloaf and mashed potatoes, Tuesday,

pork chops, fried apples. But our attentions
        are not on the meal, not on the camera, or

our mother, but on something just beyond
        the picture's border captioned with the date,

January 1960: the black-and-white
        Zenith, tuned to Davy Crockett or the Rifleman—

easy heroes. We can't know what we're armed
        against or training for—another war

for Cronkite to narrate, cataloging
        the dead nightly in a country we've not yet heard of,

or suspicious rustlings, wind in the thicket
        of his body, my brother's illness

and too-early death still years away—
        with unnumbered other captures between,

like this one: small, humorous,
        the flash from my mother's camera

caught bouncing off the wall and door behind us,
        still-sudden backlight to all we cannot see.

Vacancy

My brother claimed first the motel room
　　　we would all later share; on the farthest edge

of the farthest bed, he hunched over his guitar,
　　　the red Mustang's solid body unplugged—

his songless strumming thin, antagonistic.
　　　Just outside the door in a folding chair,

my father studied again the intricate
　　　vasculature of his map, and my mother,

who could not swim but who no doubt would have
　　　saved me anyway, looked up now

and again from her novel with a languid wave.
　　　The one it mattered to, I would have had

to beg for it—the neon *pool* glowing,
　　　moths at first dark exhausting themselves against

the humming promise of the water *vacancy*
　　　now tinted the pale green of ink—illegible.

My favorite place to be, just beneath
　　　the surface, the underwater pool lights

coming on with night. Weightless, I hovered
　　　around a dome of convex glass, a cool,

thick hemisphere not much bigger than the splay
　　　of my hand—and imagined deadlights

set into the massive hull of a ship
　　　adrift, windless, my family on its deck,

my mother's muffled call disappearing
      after them into those fathomless sources

of small light I did not want to give up,
      plenty of air yet in the joyous hold of my lungs.

Old Elementary

Terrified or furious, he would call me:
  it's in there, he'd swear, *in the old elementary—*

desperate to blame something—asbestos,
  radiation, unhappiness itself—

to place, displace the cancer onto the first school
  he despised, in the despised small town

where we grew up. I drive past it every time
  I go back, the building abandoned

years ago by all but vagrant pigeons.
  The utter childlessness of the playground

fronts it, lifeless swings, foot-worn furrows
  beneath, once slick from use, almost closed over,

a cicatrix of dandelions and wire grass.
  Then the stern-faced architecture, strict dormers,

the heavy, recessed doors through which we entered,
  two stories, walls all windows, every one

he stared out from, away from hissing radiators,
  oil-polished wood floors, crayon wax,

pencil shavings, the chronic dust of lead,
  chalk, faint fear—and the long hallways

not hard for me to imagine empty,
  dimly lit, where I recall waiting for him

one cavernous afternoon, when all
  the other children had been released, and he

was kept after, inside, *in there,* for punishment,
  in there for some small forgotten thing.

Cold Room

Her refrigerator full, my mother has stored
    some things in the cold of my brother's

closed-off room, Christmas oranges and pears
    on the floor—the salt-cured ham that hung

for a full year from the cellar rafters
    cooked now and kept on the chest of drawers.

He is far away and ill; she knows
    he will not come home, suspects

she will not see or hold him again in the flesh,
    allowed him only in smiling photographs

undone by a voice thin on the phone.
    Afternoons she climbs the slow, complaining

stairs with a platter and carving knife;
    she wears her winter coat, opens the door

to his bed still made, stale light, the scent
    of ripe fruit and cold smoke. Here, in the room

let go for this, she concentrates on carving
    the meat so even and thin she can see through it

to the blade, its clean, practiced passage—*just so,*
    she says as though to no one, *just so.*

Ground Truth

My brother's funeral over, the dark-clothed
    congregation clots the church doors, a lingering

aftermath moving into flat light—the sky
    low and swollen, a storm siren's long,

expansive notes, evenly measured,
    so loud the pauses between ring

with aftersound. Used to it, no one
    here appears alarmed, the church ladies

filing into his house bearing heavy covered
    dishes, the funeral flowers. On the muted

television tuned to the weather,
    a small area of Watch now upgrades

to Warning; the words stream across the bottom
    of the screen calling conditions perfect,

this town, this house disappeared beneath the map's
    isolated lesion, its red edges

uneven, stalled. The forecasters rely
    they say on spotters to confirm

what the radar cannot—they call it
    ground truth; until then no one knows anything

for certain beyond this inward watching.
    The room hums, an airless, crowded hive.

Their mouths are full, plates layered—fried chicken,
    deviled eggs, casseroles, bright congealed

salads with fruit suspended inside.
　　　　All of it dust. I have come here too late,

his body gone, already ash. The storm's body
　　　　could be forming now, tightening from cloud

to the gyre that will consume its path, all of it
　　　　a becoming—spiraling a wall of water,

mud, dust, and sand; with dispassion taking up
　　　　into itself the fence line, a barn—the house

beside them spared with the same dispassion. Or this,
　　　　more likely now: siren silenced, the winds

diminishing, the light, afternoon's concession
　　　　to another dusk—severe, more common truth.

Namesake

While still a child, he sensed his name—
        spoken, shouted, whispered, laughed, and called

and called and called—was not fully his,
        having been first his grandfather's, someone

his mother remembered only as a child would,
        her seat at the table his lap, his death

when she was nine, or through weary stories
        the aunts told and retold, memories the stuff

of patterned lace, fragile, impractical—
        but lasting. So—though he had come to himself

in the familiar clearing of it—he had learned
        that every time he answered or refused

its voicing over his shoulder, the name
        was not all he had to share but also

its early vanishing, and that when he did
        appear, he was near revenant and at once

perishing, impossible disappointment,
        and he could not know whom to rage against,

the one who called, the one who would not come.

Variations from the Porch

The season for it past, the porch
    had become a deep threshold

I did not want to give up
    or cross despite the cold; I learned

that I could will myself to stop
    shivering. The garden bewildered,

the birdbath was a frozen slurry
    of rainwater and the leaves

not raked, months since they fell, some still
    quick in the breeze. I don't know

what felt safe about that bleak
    reclusion, out where anyone

could have seen me; but I
    understand now that when

a bird sleeps under its own wing,
    it is the world that ceases to see.

◆

Spiders thrived there well past summer,
    surviving the shortened days,

some webs tightly made in the perfect
    symmetry of sundials

or compass roses, and some
    corner-made funnels bored smooth,

the spider hiding behind the slight
    quiescent turning, the spill of web

the mute, delicate mouth
    of a backward cornucopia.

    •

Late September blooming,
    a glorious bee-thick senescence;

the cardinal flowers I had ignored
    all summer had climbed the porch railing

to fold themselves now into needle-thin
    red sleeves of seed, and dark gray moths

thickened the abelia
    like a fever, a chill, that kind

of possession. I could hear them
    breathing with their wings.

    •

Time then came death-exhausted—
    hollowed out despite the usual

acts of vibrance. Nothing
    original about seeds dissolving

out of the possibility
    of dormancy into disappointment:

the rote bloom, known flower,
    inevitable fading

anticipated, its scent
    a sect, something it was born to.

The month my only brother died,
    mindless grief met its desire

when the confederate rose climbed high
    and deep inside the old crape myrtle—

tall and broad as a full grown maple.
    It should not yet have been blooming,

so when at last I noticed the
    something dull pink inside it—

slightly out of place and season
    intricately entwined and in full flower,

I thought first how beautiful
    it was, and then how wrong.

•

Honeysuckle had bound the quince
    from within, so I worked to find,

then follow a fragrant muscle
    as close as possible to the ground

for the cut, then pull, wrestle it out
    like an impossible tangle

from neglected hair. I knew
    I had not killed anything.

It would come back. But for the while,
    the quince breathed, red crowding

the porch and the painted-shut
    windows of the mudroom, casting

a roseglow reflection inside
  the glass; it bloomed in quiet fury

as though to please me,
  or, again, fully taken with itself.

III

Calf Killings

The first time, they were clearly slaughtered,
      dissembled in the mauling, bodies strewn
mangled over the pasture as though whatever
      attacked them had fallen into a fury
at what it did not find in them. The men
      speculated—*wolves*, they said, but there were no
wolves anymore, or *panthers*, all killed off
      long ago in the stories of dead men,

so they debated but agreed on bear—
      set traps that yawned, gleaming and clean, empty
for weeks. And so another season came
      and went before another field nearby
turned up littered with dead, though this time
      the bodies were unmarked, almost as though
they had simply lain down in their shadows
      before rain. But it must have been the calves

who had churned the frozen ground alongside
      the fenceline, worse in the corners, evidence
of a shared and violent end. The veterinarian
      could say for certain only that they had suffered
pneumonia, brought on by nights spent
      in icy rain, and while no one quite
believed it as cause, they turned to what
      was left to do, gathering the remains

to burn. The only survivor of that last night
      was a mule, moon blind and grazing calmly, ignored
old among them. But when the fire had become
      one thick, impenetrable column, the men watched
as it drifted late toward them—pulling behind it
      the rippling wake of a ragged shadow like a tedious
ghost—as though again reluctant witness,
      even to this necessary warmth.

Catfish

It nuzzles oblivion, confuses
       itself with mud. A creature

of familiar taste, it ambushes
       from its nest of ooze the pond's

brighter fish, clears its palate
       with their eggs, lumbers fat

and stagnant into winter, lulled
       into dreams of light sinking until

light drowns, and all is as before.

Documentary

After the bullet had halted in the brain
        and with it the breathing, my cousin recalls
his father slitting the hog's throat right there
        in the lot to begin the cleansing bleed.
This had happened for so many falls,
        he said the soil before the trough had been

changed by it, and while still the stuff of mud
        and sand, of hoofprints frozen into deep-cloven
molds, its color, its texture, had assumed
        a chocolaty depth, obvious, ignored
once the freshness of the smell receded into cold—
        seepage settling like a thicker rain.

     ◆

The documentary opens
        with the photograph they thought

would capture the kill—the wild boar's
        thousand-pound body strung up,

hoghook attached to the backhoe the men
        had brought into the swamp in order

to prove, measure, then bury
        this thing long-rumored, glimpsed,

heard, its size given scale
        by the man—posed smiling

as for any photograph—
        made small beside it.

•

The whole of them thriving after all,
        they appeared agreeable somehow to it—
the calm way a hog turned out roamed close
        all summer, the bell piercing its ear
unnecessary. (He reminds me that theirs
        is a hunger easily satisfied, the browsing

turning up anything that grew or landed close:
        insects, eggs, lizards, snakes, young birds,
and moles—everything rooted, bulbs and tubers,
        and with them the congregation of decay,
worms and beetles, a lung-shot doe some hunter
        gave up following discovered with equal delight.)

It entered the lot without real protest,
        showing joy in the slop and corn, the confines
of the trough. Perhaps an understanding came
        in the suckling, that the afterworld of their bodies
was fused with the ones turned feral, escaped to the hidden
        sounders and the wild odor of the hive.

•

The narrative, already virile,
        the town nearby embellished—

how he heard before he saw it,
        killed it with a single shot

or surely it would have killed him—
        how the creature had all the features

of a wild boar in its sheer size,
        the coat mud-rimed wire, tusks thick

as a man's forearm, but also how
        it bore sure signs that someone had once

owned it, claimed it in the docked tail,
        in the ear's notch—deep, deliberate.

                ◆

My mother says the day was decided
        after a week's worth of heavy frost,
persimmons stricken sweet, the dawn
        shadowless. The axe angled gnomon-like
but hourless from the block. Smoke
        from the scalding fire so finely laced
the air it was as inextricable
        from it as the sound of a blade

sharpening, its measure breathlike, the fragrance
        of a whetted edge mingling iron
with the smoke. The world outside the pen
        was slatted again, redefined in thick slices
of dawn, and with its slow reemergence
        of color, the tattered remnants of the garden

returned. The sage patch still dense by the woodshed
        volunteered thicker and healthier
every year—and the house from which the children
        spilled with slop and corn, their screams coming sharp,
voices rising, pale wisps feathering
        from the heat of small, determined mouths.

                ◆

The town celebrated, paraded,
        the children wearing plastic snouts

and little ears, holding paper cones
        of cotton candy, greasy sacks

of popcorn. Following the marching band,
        someone's tractor pulled a float

that carried a living tableau
  of the scene they had been told

they could stop imagining:
  a blood-covered man overcome

by the long-feared boar—in paper mâché
  a quick, rough rendering.

                    ◆

All of it was worth the work she says:
      nothing wasted—hocks, hams, chops, fatback,
bacon, even the ears, feet, intestine,
      tongue, the heart, even the brain that would be
in the morning scrambled to the plural *brains-*
      and-eggs, salted, peppered; her mother
shushing the children not to think about it.
      The learned ritual of that day would define

winter—the body going from fall's quick,
      purgatorial fattening to an anatomy
segmented, ordered first in the meatbox, hams
      and shoulders packed tight in salt, kept in the hold
of the smokehouse, where later they would be hung, crowded there;
      she says its eaves steamed night after night
against the early winter sky—a small house
      that would not succumb to the fire it had inside it.

                    ◆

But doubt would suspend the story,
  possibility upon

whispered possibility,
  then a small certain voice,

then two: they could have mistaken it
  for the one still in the swamp,

something they had never known.
  Only three men saw the body

after all, and them not from
  around here, the photograph

a made thing—no proof
  in such small witness.

  •

So much revision in the rendering, in the precise
  economy of a slow, graveless decay,
some of what remained of the body distilled,
  disappeared in the snaps and potatoes—seasoned
the greens, the soup, assumed the form of lard
  in the bucket, of soap by the sink. Relics of the body

once carried, obeyed, the feet, cloven and delicate,
  my mother learned to pickle alongside
cucumbers, beets, and peaches; no longer gravity
  bound, they floated weightless, suspended in the gallon
glass jar like curiosities in a medical museum—
  or specimens preserved for study.

  •

And so the documentary
  closes with the men's

return, scientists
  among them this time.

They wear rubber gloves,
  boots to the hip, black

masks. No resurrection, this—
  inquiry an insult

to the swamp's slow recollection
of what has already

disappeared among them,
the fact of that.

.

It drifts through the dead finish of the thicket—
swamp and understory—shared threshold
with predictable clearings, lots, coops,
cellars, lofts, and cages, a house, the shadows
neat, obedient. One form reforms,
resolves, survival more than the memory

of muscle and space, more than the summoning
back of time, the body and brain indivisible,
changing around what has changed and will
again, penumbral noon and after
noon, the way the wind rises as something
recalled, called, and recalled.

IV

The Porch

This is not illness, not yet dying,
      this stillness a changed way

of being here on the porch. Ninety-three,
      my father sits much as he always sat,

still recognizable as himself, baseball cap
      the same, rocking chair, the flyswatter,

old defense he holds but will not use,
      its mesh a small window screen

keeping nothing away from him. The wrens
      have chosen again the glazed-clay bird bottle

he hung close under the shadowy eaves
      and have more quickly accepted him, his presence

so little to grow accustomed to as they fly
      back and forth, above and around him in ordinary

industry; in their beaks pieces of straw,
      tufts of moss or spider's web, they pause

now and then to light on the clothesline,
      the downspout, the back of his rocker.

When one wren grips the bill of his cap the way
      it will in a few minutes land on a dogwood branch,

I understand that although I am as still
      as he is, and that such concentration

is its own disappearance, the birds
      must sense the difference, his being so fully formed

it has become unquestioned part
      of the small landscape of their survival.

Dial Variations

The longer my father lives, the smaller
      the task my mother gives him—

scissors to sharpen, the carving knife;
      whetstone balanced on his knees,

he hones a blade for an hour.

          •

The sundial rises from its tangled
      bed of herbs, fragrant even

in winter's reversible death. A bird
      drinks from the small sheer pond

of its rain-shimmering face, from its own
      reflection, the wind-shirred sky's.

          •

Once a week she helps him
      into the living room where he opens

the oval glass face of the calendar
      clock to wind it with its brass key.

Two more times she will have to
      remind him to give or take back

the hour whose loss or gain he has
      grown accustomed to, as dusk

coming early, or light lingering.

•

Ice-occluded, then, birdless,
      the face has frozen into an eye's

milk-thick cataract. Aphasic
      the hours unaccounted for—

The Present Tense

There will be a worse day. He will live long
      enough not to know me at all, and the turn

toward it, begun this hour with recognition,
      has slowed to a measureless stare, worse

than the wordless pauses common now;
      he concentrates on me, direct and quiet,

the way light concentrates, falling through
      a window to the floor. I hold his gaze

until I am considering the surface
      of his eyes the way I might the dulling

surface of a pond drought-shrunken, clouded
      over with dust and pollen. But there is light

enough to see my face mirrored
      weakly, small, infant in the pupils

as though from some great distance. Finally, I ask him
      what he is thinking about—or if he is

remembering something he'd like to tell me,
      and at last he nods saying yes, he is; he is

remembering his daughter, naming me
      in the third person as though I am not

the one asking, as though I am the one—not dying,
      but already mourned, and he has survived me

long enough to find solace in a memory.
      And I, as I have always known myself,

am fallen away then from the present
      tense into reminiscence—the lucid *was*.

I

The brain seizes on it, familiar
      beginning of what he means to say, the rest

of the sentence urgently close, utterly
      lost—the body of something dissevered

from its head; so, worrying the hem
      of his pajama jacket like a rosary between

forefinger and thumb, he tries again
      and again, repeating the long flat *i*—

a needle deepening in the groove—until
      his voice registers something beyond grief,

disbelief, the word having returned
      to sound—oblivious elegy, that pure vowel.

Refusal

My mother spoon-feeds him a vanilla milkshake,
    and, though hesitant, he opens his mouth

out of habit. His last spring is happening
    outside, and from the final morning

in this house, his body leans toward the window,
    a posture reminiscent of the old compulsion

to see something he loved, finches troubling
    the feeder for the last of the thistle

my mother will give them—winter almost over.
    The multiple perches too few, the birds

compete for them, the long cylinder plumbing
    the vivid midst of the flock's relentless chaos,

a brilliant gold ravening, willful
    and tense. His mouth closing becomes his only

no, refusing what he can, to turn his head
    away from them, the milky cool of the spoon.

Then

From the edge of his bed and the sill of a long afternoon,
      I look out at a wind too mean for April,

the muted edge of weather worse somewhere else
      whetting itself against the window;

the trees struggle against it, a bird's flight
      useless argument. People lean

into and away from it, bright clothes
      blown tight against their bodies.

His brief emersions ended, my father
      will not surface again from that other

place, his being defined by cycles of anguished
      breathing followed by the shallow and sparse—

phases of what appears to be sleep
      with agitation, the unconscious

physical despair of nightmare, this
      dying like giving birth, the labor of it

that long, intense, inexorable.
      He works his hands into a knot so cold

and frozen-strong I cannot undo it, the flesh
      eerily translucent, a tangible

invisibility through which I see
      as though through glass the thinning

blue veins, the tendons' course along the bone,
      the fact of the bone itself undeniable beginning

of our seeing past this place, the shadows' slant
      dissolving, the night shift coming on.

The Hearing

The nurses shout into the labyrinth
    of his ear long after he stops answering,

telling us to keep talking to him, too,
    that the hearing is the last to go:

All my life he loved to tell this story
    about Marshall, a neighbor boy

he'd been in school with—pale, fevered
    six-year-old, and how he had sat

right behind him, close enough to hear
    the tubercular wheeze in between

the coughing everyone heard, close enough
    to see the blood bright in his handkerchief

before he was kept home and no one saw him
    anymore. And he remembered the first

summer after Marshall died, the grieving
    mother coming over to them at the church

revival picnic, her stony appraisal of him
    and, as though he had no more hearing than a mule

standing there, saying out loud to his mother—
    Kate, you'll never raise him; he looks just like Marshall

did the year before he died, as though death
    had somehow made her expert—and prophet.

And he had run, afraid, out of hearing,
    past the stunted, consumptive plots,

the graveyard lambs, toward the men beginning
       to cut the watermelon that had been floating

all day weightless in the spring pool, the knife cleaving
       the dense, glistening green-marbled body that fell

rocking into perfect halves like lungs
       healthy pink, and he took breath after

deep breath to spit out seeds, like those words,
       slick, dark, unheard—as he would tell, and tell it.

Cause

We dress him for the fire in what he might have
    chosen for himself. Arranging neckties

on the bed, bright-shimmering as a peacock's
    display, we match, consider, consult—busying

ourselves. The forms we have already filled out
    in duplicate, triplicate, the death certificate

ordered—rote questions, designated
    lines for time and cause, time itself

not among the choices, the *failure*
    to thrive standard they explain, a diagnosis

I've heard before but only for the newborn
    that refuse without cause to suckle.

We have found his birth certificate
    in the labyrinth of a desk that had been

his father's before him, tight pigeonholes
    and boxes within drawers, the bottom one

as deep as a baby's crib, laden
    with banknotes, ledgers, vaccination records,

deeds, loans, pocket knives, dogtags, tax returns,
    eyeglasses, a fist-thick bunch of keys—

vanished doors—all of it a catalog
    of balances, the satisfied, useless,

broken, sentimental, saved for no real
    purpose but this, the cluttered consolation

of ended causes, the hours that do not burn.

V

Mortmain

All over town even the most genteel
    houses have trained roses to climb a trellis,

allowed wisteria a porch railing,
    ivy a chimney, a wall. Sometimes, from houses

where the very old still live, neglected vines
    will have spread, if not in a willful spill

along the ground, then over it, crossing
    the street on a telephone wire, slow news.

But on the outskirts, where the houses begin
    to thin out toward farmland, one is so overcome,

no one recalls it otherwise, the consumption
    a confluence of honeysuckle, trumpet vine,

morning glory, kudzu, wisteria;
    only the chimney rises recognizable

as though above high water. By early summer,
    the front porch has become another room

given fully to it, walls all curtain,
    falling veil a dense, nerved weave of leaves

and bees, confusion of wind and wingbeat,
    penumbral patterns of light. The kudzu

escaped the highway, had to have crossed two miles
    and the train trestle, but the rest was by someone's

common design, daylilies and spiderwort
    delighting themselves in evanescent blooming

that lasts all summer. The old can't name
        the last to live here, ownership unclear,

whose title, whose fault—and so even children
        have grown unafraid of a storyless

and ghostless space; all of us so accustomed,
        we fail often to see it, awash in green

as the yards around, what was pasture, the bordering
        stand of trees part of its vanishing from us.

When summer's course cools like lava flow,
        vines fade—a waxlike backward melting

that bruises before settling to gray.
        In the same way an image rises

from the negative to print, the porch
        appears, then, a chair, a doorless frame,

a window. The air cold, though, we hurry past,
        our faith absolute that summer again

will come to cross and enclose winter's aperture,
        and we will no longer be able to see

in far enough to see the soot-rimmed socket
        where the stovepipe went, clothes hanger on a nail,

a glove, the faint trespass of a neighbor's
        woodsmoke, or our own—barest, hesitant specter.

Jubilation

for Betty Adcock

The rear wall of her house all glass, the garden
    defined the living room with its small stand

of paper birches, a narrow stream, the hillside
    that confined it—all quick with flight and shadows

of flight—cardinals, thrushes, juncos, doves,
    sometimes a heron, a hawk. She said

the birds must believe, if belief applied in such,
    that the mirrored trees were ahead when they flew

into the reflection that was her house,
    unaware that what killed or stunned was more

than glass—the misdirected flight we all
    take sometimes into the place just left behind.

And when she found a bird tangled in ivy,
    she put it in a shoebox in a closet;

there sometimes it would return to itself—
    the enclosed hour she had come to imagine

it perceived only as a healing fugue
    of darkness, another night that had indeed

passed not so much unlike all the others.
    The lid removed then not to death

but to sudden afternoon and the briefest
    moment of stillness before the rush

of lifting up and out, a quickening
    reabsorbed at once into the oblivion

of a world having gone on bright and raucous
        without it, no worse for the absence, perhaps—

but surely that was jubilation she heard
        in the cicadas' immediate flourish

of sound, as though the hour itself had been
        restored with the bird it had moved through.

Arterial

I would not have heard him ring the bell,
      but would know he had rung it, waking

to the aftersound of my mother downstairs,
      getting up to see what my father

needed, sleeping in the guestroom.
      He bought that bell years ago at auction

when the old hotel was to be torn down.
      So much of what was being sold redundant—

ordinary lamps and bedframes—the brass
      dome of the bell was small but singular,

a distinct, shining hemisphere shared
      by strangers sounding the one note to summon

the clerk for a room, a night or two. This visit,
      though, we are again alone in the house,

my father dead a year—my mother, now able
      to sleep through the night, asleep, the bell

in a chest of drawers. The sound I have confused
      with her slippers shushing along the hallway's

hardwood floor—indistinguishable from it—
      my own pulse, sleepless push of blood.

For Once

I had many times walked past it: crowded
    stand of mixed woods where a field used to be,

self-ordained survivors of a place
    having gone unnoticed long enough

for them to volunteer: maples, scrub pines,
    some cedars—a blood beech leaved even

in winter, little remarkable either
    for ruin or beauty. And then something, in there,

caused me to pause, sounds a wakeful house
    can make—the restlessness of a slumberous

body shifting in bed, the strike of a match,
    foot doubtful on a stair, kindling catching,

water from a spigot, fatwood hiss.
    Or all of it the acoustics of emptiness—

needles of ice ticking on abandoned glass,
    a porch swing's chained keening. But it was habit

to find the familiar in that shifting architecture,
    its trueness not finally in the measure

and level of some human past, or possible,
    but in that present quickening—wind-cast

shadows of sound and soundlessness, unseen,
    unknowable, and, for once, enough.

Lifeguard

She perches high on the stand, gleaming whistle
        dangling, on her suit a dutiful,

faded red cross. Mine her only life
        to guard, she does for a while watch

the middle-aged woman who has nothing better
        to do than swim laps in the Y's indoor pool

on a late Friday afternoon. I am slow,
        though, boring, length after predictable

length of breaststroke or the duller lap
        of elementary backstroke perfectly

executed within the taut confines
        of the brightly buoyed lane. So she abandons me

to study split-ends, hangnail, wristwatch,
        until—the body of the whistle cupped

loosely in her palm—her head nods toward
        shallow dreams. I've never felt so safe in my life,

making flawless, practiced turns, pushing, invisible,
        to reenter my own wake, reverse it.

Flocking Theory

At dusk each winter evening, in the half hour
  before they must relinquish sky to night,

starlings quicken, flock in forms—symmetries
  shifting—the likenesses so fast and fluid

I can't hold on to any one before
  it dissolves into another, and I

have taught myself to accept the seamless
  recreations not as uneasy

whimsy but as the musings of a lucid soul
  or the disclosures of God: the wind

itself made seen, the shade a shadow casts.
  No one knows for certain what controls this,

the flock moving by space measured and kept—
  strict distances—between the bodies.

But the birds, I like to think, are having
  none of theory, anyway, whatever

it may be, none of me, abandoning
  themselves instead to the invariable

bliss of what is, the fact of flying
  manifest in every changing figure:

one enormous wing, a waterfall
  of bees, a murmurous curtain falling

to rise as smoke, a funnel cloud,
  helix, an arm, its empty sleeve.

CPSIA information can be obtained at www.ICGtesting.com
Printed in the USA
LVOW07s1847161214

419117LV00009B/1099/P

...stly likenesses of children in postmortem photog... small-town businesses gone under—remnants of the interstate's... of uranium beneath a plot of local farmland, these poems reckon with losses both personal an... communal. This is a hauntingly beautiful collection from a poet attentive to measure and the way... of things in both the natural and man-made worlds to reveal to us 'musings of a lucid soul / or th... disclosures of God.'"—NATASHA TRETHEWEY

"*Secure the Shadow* may seem to be about death, the brother's death, the father's death, everyone... death. Yet the poems themselves, graceful, sturdy, fiercely controlled, profoundly imaged, are th... poet's brilliant argument for life. With realism and dignity, she balances pain and grief word by wor... to arrive at startling wisdom and extraordinary freedom. A beautiful, beautiful book that sounds th... depths of love."—KELLY CHERRY

"I really do not know of another writer of her generation who can weave such diverse materials to... gether to make such a cohesive and urgent whole. With *Secure the Shadow*, Emerson once again prove... that she is among our essential poets."—DAVID WOJAHN

"With superb artistry and a cool, but never cold, eye, Emerson sublimates her grief into elegant elegy... unsentimental and unforgettable—as when, driving past a house fire's 'bright-rising / enravishment... she does 'not stop to watch someone else's / tragedy burn past this brief, nearly / beautiful suspensio... that changes nothing.'"—ANDREW HUDGINS

Daringly realistic and artfully mediated by past and present, Claudia Emerson's *Secure the Shadow*... contains historical pieces as well as poems centering on the deaths of the poet's brother and father... Emerson covers all aspects of the tragedies that, as Keats believed, contribute to our human collec... tive of *Soul-making*, in which each death accrues into an immortal web of ongoing love and meaning... for the living. Emerson's unwavering gaze shows that loss cannot be eluded, but can be embraced ir... elegies as devastating as they are beautiful.

The macabre title poem refers to the old custom of making daguerreotypes, primitive photographs... of deceased loved ones. Other striking poems describe animal deaths—mysterious calf killings, ... hog slaughter, the burial of a dead jay, "identifiable / but light, dry, its eyes vacant orbits."

Death, as the speaker's heart and mind instruct her, exists in a shadow world. When the body dis... appears, the shadow also flees. By securing the shadow, the poet finds a representation of the dead'... soul, a soul always linked to the body. Hence, Emerson's attention to the minute details of the body'... repose—reflected in the long, related sequence of refrained poems—never allows its memory to fade

CLAUDIA EMERSON's five books include *Late Wife*, winner o... Pulitzer Prize, and most recently, *Figure Studies*. Emerson has ... awarded fellowships from the National Endowment for the Arts... Library of Congress, and the Guggenheim Foundation. Former ... laureate of Virginia, she holds the Arrington Distinguished Ch... Poetry at the University of Mary Washington in Virginia.

Southern Messenger Poets | Dave Smith, Series Editor

LOUISIANA STATE UNIVERSITY PRESS
BATON ROUGE 70803
www.lsupress.org

ISBN 978-0-8071-4303-2